East Anglian Steam Gallery

INTRODUCTION

The popularity of previous albums in this series, coupled with the emergence of further exciti[...] steam journey in pictures around the Eastern Counties.

High standards within these pages necessitated long hours in the darkroom, and situatio[...] hundred eggs in the hope that one will hatch" have occurred more than once. However, with[...] the task was far from arduous.

To hopefully cater for most East Anglian steam devotees I have endeavoured to balance the selection geographically, at the same time covering as many different locomotive classes as possible, majoring on those of particular historical interest, at locations (within photographic limitations) not featured to any great extent in other publications.

The former London, Tilbury & Southend lines, recorded on film in tremendous detail by Frank Church, qualifies for extra coverage, along with the Midland & Great Northern, an early casualty within our system (125 miles of this admirable railway closed "en-bloc" in 1959); today, it still evokes fond memories and fervent interest amongst the modelling fraternity.

We also visit areas that have "lost their former identity" through electrification and modernisation, branches closed during the Beeching cutbacks, plus views included solely on the grounds of quality.

To complement the Frank Church collection, I have included prints by other photographers whose work I hope to feature in future publications, a "sampler" for exciting material which is largely unpublished.

John D. Mann, Frinton-on-Sea, 1989

ACKNOWLEDGEMENTS

In the production of *East Anglian Steam Gallery – Part Three* I have relied heavily on the Frank Church Collection for the majority of photographs included. Access to these unique scenes has again been possible by kind permission of Peter Snell, Photograph Officer, Essex Bus Enthusiasts Group, to whom I am eternally grateful.

I would like to thank my colleagues Win Cole and Geoff Griggs for contributions and assistance received; also Roy Yeomans, R. K. (Mac) McKenny, M. J. Fox, Dr. W. J. Naunton, and the dedicated staff of the Lavenham Press Ltd. My thanks also to all correspondents who purchased and enjoyed "Part Two", in particular Mr. D. Pepperell who spotted a small error in captions on page one. The photographs reproduced on the front cover and introduction page were in fact taken on the same day, August 7th 1958.

FRONT COVER
SOUTHEND CENTRAL – November 9th 1958. Steam supreme at an Essex resort. "Standard" Class 4MT tanks Nos 80102, 80101 and 80077 pose in the Autumn sunshine between duties.   (*Photo:* F. Church)

INSIDE FRONT COVER
SHOEBURYNESS – Spring 1951. A general view with the Motive Power Depot visible left of picture. A train is leaving for Fenchurch Street.
(*Photo:* F. Church)

BACK COVER
HATFIELD – April 30th 1955. Immaculate Class B12/3 No 61576 after arrival with the "HERTS RAILTOUR". The fireman is about to remove the headboard.
(*Photo:* R. K. McKenny)

THIS PAGE
FERRY – October 4th 1958. Midland & Great Northern memories! A self-explanatory notice recorded shortly before closure of this legendary East Anglian railway.   (*Photo:* F. Church)

Copyright and design, South Anglia Productions, Frinton-on-Sea, Essex.
Published by South Anglia Productions, 26 Rainham Way, Frinton-on-Sea, Essex C013 9NS
ISBN 1 871277 02 7
Printed in England by The Lavenham Press Ltd.

SOUTHEND CENTRAL – July 5th 1959. "Crab" (Hughes/Fowler) L.M.S. design 2–6–0 No 42870 passes under the old signal gantry at the approaches to the station with an excursion from the L.M.R. on a perfect summer's day. (*Photo:* F. Church)

SOUTHEND VICTORIA – October 15th 1959. Steam under the wires. In "D.C." electrification days Liverpool Street/Shenfield (Class "306") stock provides interest as Thompson design Class L1 tank No 67735 leaves on a parcels train.

(*Photo*: F. Church)

SHOEBURYNESS – Summer 1951. A delightful study of Ex-L.T.S. tank No 41969 on shunting duties at Shoeburyness carriage sidings. Activities of this class were not confined to former L.T.S. lines. Three members of the class were based at Colchester during the mid-fifties and could be seen at work regularly at Clacton–Walton and Ipswich.

(*Photo:* F. Church)

BETWEEN LEIGH-ON-SEA AND CHALKWELL – December 29th 1959. Gresley design Class J39/2 (with standard 4200 gallon tender) No 64951 is running tender first on a works train during drainage operations between the two stations. Note the dilapidated fogman's box in the foreground.

(*Photo*: F. Church)

NARROW ROAD DRIVE SLOWLY

LEIGH-ON-SEA – December 22nd 1959. A damp winter's day heightens the atmosphere of this superb scene. "Stanier" three cylinder Class 4 tank No 42524 runs round. The through London line is in the foreground. Note the "sand-drag" (front of loco) providing extra protection on a siding close to running tracks.

(*Photo:* F. Church)

APPROACHING PITSEA JUNCTION – February 16th 1958. Another J39/2 No 64957 is recorded heading a ballast train through harsh winter sunlight.

(*Photo:* F. Church)

SHELLHAVEN – March 15th 1952. The 12.20 pm (Sats only) train to Tilbury Riverside waits to leave headed by "Whitelegg" L.T.S. 0–6–2 tank No 41984. Note the ex-L.T.S. coaches with footboards. (*Photo*: F. Church)

TILBURY – July 18th 1959. A view of the motive power depot looking towards Southend. A leaky "W.D." No 90063 is in the foreground.
(*Photo*: F. Church)

PURFLEET – September 1st 1958. A goods train for West Thurrock stands in the station hauled by another "Whitelegg" L.T.S. tank No 41992 (water tank cover open). The platform is lit by gas. *(Photo:* F. Church)

WEST THURROCK JUNCTION – May 8th 1960. The signalman of junction signalbox hands over the "staff" to the driver of "Standard" tank No 80075, heading a Fenchurch Street train via the Ockendon branch.

(*Photo*: F. Church)

NEAR OCKENDON – November 30th 1958. Autumn mist surrounds "W.D." No 90034 as it prepares to leave for the next hole boring site during electrification work. The cementing train waits in the background, near Ockendon Station. Washing day seems unaffected by the presence of two steam engines!

(*Photo*: F. Church)

OCKENDON – May 20th 1957. "Ivatt" G. N. Design Class "C12" 4–4–2 tank No 67363 and Class N7/3 No 69691 leave with Upminster and Grays "auto" trains. (*Photo*: F. Church)

OCKENDON – May 20th 1957. Class N7/3 No 69691 leaves for Upminster with an "auto" train. The lattice footbridge and wickerwork basket barrow positioned under the steps are of interest. (*Photo:* F. Church)

UPMINSTER – May 20th 1957. A fine array of semaphore signals feature in this view of N7/3 69691 passing the East signalbox with a Grays "auto" train. Lineside detail, especially point rodding shows up well.
(*Photo*: F. Church)

BARKING – April 12th 1958. Class N7/3 No 69709 is nicely turned out propelling the Ipswich District Engineers' Saloon into the station (destination unknown). (*Photo:* F. Church)

BARKING – December 29th 1956. Class 9F No 92108 is working tender first with a coal train on a murky winter's day.
(*Photo:* F. Church)

ONGAR – July 1st 1957. A view of Class "F5" No 67200 with the Epping "auto" train near the end of steam. Although situated close to London this part of Essex remained largely rural until the late "Fifties". Note the point locks, and the poster on the platform buildings. (*Photo*: F. Church)

CAMBRIDGE – July 6th 1961. Standard Class 4 2–6–0 No 76031 is pulling away from the station with the 08.10 train to March. (*Photo*: M. J. Fox)

CAMBRIDGE – March 3rd 1961. L.M.S. "Black 5" No 45393 leaves on a goods train for Bletchley on a bright morning.

(*Photo*: M. J. Fox)

GODMANCHESTER – June 14th 1958. "Ivatt" Class 2 No 46495 is almost "silhouetted" in this lovely scene. A train comprised of Midland stock is pictured just after leaving for Kettering, crossing the River Ouse. Note the holidaymakers and caravans in the distance. *(Photo:* F. Church)

HUNTINGDON (EAST) – June 14th 1958. "Riddles" B.R. Standard Class 2 No 78020 enters East station with a passenger train for Kettering. A G.W. Siphon F is attached at the rear. A wealth of detail for railway modellers in this photograph.
(*Photo*: F. Church)

NORTHAMPTON (CASTLE) – August 15th 1958. A brief excursion into Northants. A "Stanier" Class 5MT approaches past the impressive signalbox, with a passenger train. (*Photo:* F. Church)

PETERBOROUGH – August 9th 1958. Class "K3" No 61970 is seen running down to East station from the G.N. main line. Tracks to the left are for the Nene Valley.

(*Photo:* F. Church)

PETERBOROUGH (EAST) – August 19th 1958. "Stanier" 8F No 48185 leaves with a short goods train. Note the interesting and complicated trackwork.

(*Photo:* F. Church)

BOURNE – October 18th 1958. A view at the Saxby end of the station. "Gresley" Class K2 No 61771 is taking water.

(Photo: F. Church)

SPALDING – August 9th 1958. "Ivatt" Class 4MT No 43090 is approaching with a train from the M.&G.N. section. There are two level crossings and unusual architecture to be observed in this view.

(*Photo:* F. Church)

HOLBEACH – August 9th 1958. A Midland & Gt. Northern scene so representative of East Anglian post-war rail travel. A Midland design "4F" No 44122 arrives with a through train to Gt. Yarmouth.

(*Photo:* F. Church)

SUTTON BRIDGE – October 4th 1958. A brilliantly sunny day and Class J6 No 64250 has just arrived with a train from Spalding. Frank's photography at its very best, and a scene far removed from rural train travel of today.

(*Photo*: F. Church)

TYDD – October 4th 1958. More M.&G.N. memories. 4MT No 43094 with a passenger train for Peterborough.

(*Photo*: F. Church)

TYDD – October 4th 1958. Class "4MT" No 43094 crosses the single track bridge with a train for Peterborough. Note the 61' 6" Gresley eight Compartment coach behind loco. (*Photo*: F. Church)

SOUTH LYNN – October 4th 1958. Class J6 No 64265 is running round on a damp overcast day. Here, the M.&G.N. system joined the G.E. terminus by means of a loop. Ironically, a new modern locomotive shed at this location had only just been completed when the line closed. Note also the varied collection of wagons and the signal gantry. (*Photo*: F. Church)

FAKENHAM (WEST) – August 8th 1958. A smartly turned out 4MT No 43150 stands with a South Lynn train. The lattice footbridge and fencing completes a well attended appearance at a location now bereft of railways.

(*Photo*: F. Church)

POTTER HEIGHAM – August 7th 1958. Another typical M.&G.N. country scene, although this location was one of Broadland's principal stations. Class 4MT No 43160 is seen running tender first on a train of three Gresley (61' 6") vehicles. Note the unattended suitcase on the platform. What sinister overtones might it pose today!

(*Photo*: F. Church)

NORWICH (VICTORIA) – March 31st 1962. The "Great Eastern Commemorative Railtour" hauled by "Britannia" No 70003 "John Bunyan". Certain local services had used this station until May 1916, after which it was used as a goods depot only. This tour celebrated the amalgamation in 1862 of the Eastern Counties Railway and other small companies to form the "Great Eastern". 70003 hauled the train from London to Norwich Victoria; a diesel shunter was coupled for the short journey to Norwich (Thorpe) with the Pacific at the rear! After trips over cross-country and branches with a "J17" in charge, the "Britannia" came back on at Thetford for the return journey via Ely and Cambridge. A memorable day!

(Photo: R. K. McKenny)

NORWICH (THORPE) – Late 1960s. Preserved A3 No 4472 "Flying Scotsman" visited Norwich several times on special trains during this period. Thousands of spectators turned out to witness a fleeting return to steam power. The loco is seen backing down to the platform after turning on the Wensum Triangle (turntable facilities having been removed – see *E.A. Steam Gallery, Part One*, page 19). "4472"'s specially constructed tender (no longer used) can be clearly seen.

(*Photo*: G. Griggs.)

NORWICH (THORPE) – August 15th 1959. An amazing "triple-header" arrives on a summer evening. Class D16/3 No 62511 leads an unidentified class "B1", plus another D16/3 No 62544. This unusual formation was probably due to the traffic density, the locos returning to the terminus during a busy holiday period. (*Photo:* R. A. Yeomans)

YARMOUTH (VAUXHALL) – August 15th 1959. A passenger train approaches headed by Class "K3" No 61918 piloting a Class D16/3. (*Photo:* R. A. Yeomans)

YARMOUTH BEACH – August 1948. An Ivatt Class "D2" No 2152 seen here in store. It is doubtful if it saw further service before being withdrawn in January 1949, without receiving the B.R. "6" prefix. Built by the G.N.R. in 1898, 2152 was one of several sent to the M.&G.N. line in 1936/7, replacing that company's elderly 4–4–0s scrapped when the L.N.E.R. took over working the line

(Photo: R. K. McKenny)

BECCLES – May 28th 1960. Enthusiasts are very much in evidence, occupying windows during an M.&G.N. Society railtour, hauled by an immaculate J15 No 65469. The movable platform, a hallmark of the East Suffolk line, is in the foreground. *(Photo: Dr. W. J. Naunton)*

BECCLES – 1958. Class N7/3 No 69708 is seen on a local train. This engine was one of two class members fitted with "Whittaker" tablet apparatus for working the M.&G.N. between Melton Constable and Cromer. 69708 ended her varied career at Colchester in deplorable condition working mostly on the Walton branch until withdrawal in January 1961. Note the G.E. semaphore.

(*Photo:* R. A. Yeomans)

IPSWICH – July 12th 1959. The last Class D16/3 to remain in service, No 62613 calls with the "L.C.G.B. Eastern Counties Limited Railtour". The engine was withdrawn in 1960; sadly no D16/3s were saved for preservation.　　　　(*Photo:* Dr. W. J. Naunton)

BELSTEAD BANK (Nr. Ipswich) – April 3rd 1976. A crisp early Spring morning and preserved Class "S15" No 841 "Greene King" is setting out with the first of its sadly ill-fated rail tours. The newly created B.R. Manningtree–March steamroute was eventually abandoned after aborted journeys due to mechanical failure. On this occasion "841" looked magnificent and provided a fine spectacle pounding towards Ipswich, having been completely restored by a dedicated team based at the Stour Valley R.P.S. (now East Anglian Railway Museum). *(Photo: J. D. Mann)*

CLACTON-ON-SEA – October 13th 1957. A pre-electrification view looking towards Colchester. Class B17/6 No 61630 "Tottenham Hotspur" awaits departure. Note the "Trade Bike" and P. W. work in progress.

(*Photo*: F. Church)

SUDBURY – July 31st 1958. Class "E4" No 62785 leaves with a Colchester bound train, looking very smart in the summer sunshine. In this unusual angle the loco's tender cab can be clearly seen. Remaining members of this class were very active over the Stour Valley line in their final years, this route providing some fairly heavy work for these elderly 2–4–0s. On withdrawal in December 1959, 62785 was completely restored to its G.E.R. livery.

(Photo: F. Church)

BURY ST. EDMUNDS – September 6th 1953. The "East Anglian Railtour", having been duly recorded, is rejoined by enthusiasts enjoying this "R.C.T.S." organised "special". Class "J20" No 64685 took over at Marks Tey and worked through to Cambridge via Sudbury and Bury St. Edmunds.

(Photo: R. K. McKenny)

WITHAM – August 10th 1958. Class "J19" No 64656 has just arrived with the "Northern and Eastern Railtour", having worked from Liverpool Street via Bishop's Stortford, Dunmow and Braintree. The loco then ran tender first to Marks Tey. (The line between Bishop's Stortford and Braintree had been closed to passenger traffic since March 1952.)

(*Photo*: R. K. McKenny)

WICKHAM BISHOPS – April 21st 1958. The ultimate branch line atmosphere is captured in this beautiful photograph of Class "F5" No 67214 departing with a Maldon train.

(Photo: F. Church)

INGATESTONE – November 3rd 1958. Class "B1" No 61264 has surplus steam shortly after passing through with a goods train in the Chelmsford direction, on a dreary late Autumn day. (*Photo*: F. Church)

SHENFIELD. December 20th, 1958. A misty Winter's day and Class "B1" No 61110 waits with a parcels train.

(Photo: E. Church)

COPPER MILL JUNCTION – Autumn 1951. A football match is in progress (right of picture) as Class "D16/3" No 62585 runs tender first past the signalbox with a goods train.

(*Photo*: F. Church)

LIVERPOOL STREET – March 29th 1958. Class "B17/6" No 61623 "Lambton Castle" and the first Brush Type 2 (Class 31/0) D5500 stand in the sulphurous air of the terminus awaiting turns of duty

(*Photo*: F. Church)